THE WONDERS OF OUR WORLD

Rocks & Minerals

Neil Morris

CRABTREE PUBLISHING COMPANY

www.crabtreebooks.com

The Wonders of our World

Crabtree Publishing Company

PMB 16A
350 Fifth Avenue,
Suite 3308
New York, NY 10118

616 Welland Avenue
St. Catharines, Ontario
Canada
L2M 5V6

73 Lime Walk
Headington, Oxford
OX3 7AD
United Kingdom

Author: Neil Morris
Managing editor: Jackie Fortey
Editors: Penny Clarke & Greg Nickles
Designer: Richard Rowan
Production manager: Chris Legee
Picture research: Robert Francis

Picture Credits:
Artists: Ray Burrow 7, 9, 11, 13, 14, 15, 18, 20, 23, 25;
Peter Dennis 22, 28; Deborah Johnson 19; Paul Williams 4.
Photographs: R.A. Fortey 28; Robert Francis, 3 (title page),
5 (top and bottom right), 8, 10, 10-11 (bottom), 11, 16-17,
17, 20-21, 22-23, 29 (left); Robert Harding Picture Library
5 (left), 7, 8-9, 13, 18, 19 (bottom left), 24, 24-25 (bottom),
26, 26-27, 29 (right); Hutchison Picture Library 12, 15, 22,
24-25 (top); Caroline Jones 6, 6-7, 16; The Natural History
Museum, London 19 (top), 27; Science Photo Library 21;
Isabella Tree 19 (bottom right). All other photographs by
Digital Stock and Digital Vision.

Cataloging-in-publication data

Morris, Neil
      Rocks and minerals
p. cm. — (The wonders of our world)
Includes index.
ISBN 0-86505-835-0 (library bound) ISBN 0-86505-847-4 (pbk).
An introduction to rocks and minerals, and their types, origins,
and uses.
1. Rocks and minerals—Juvenile literature. 2. Minerals—
Juvenile literature. [1. Rocks. 2. Minerals.] I. Title. II. Series:
Morris, Neil. Wonders of our world.

QE432.2.M67 1998   j552   LC 98-3307 CIP

© 1998 Snapdragon Publishing Ltd.
Created and Produced by Snapdragon Publishing Ltd in con-
junction with Crabtree Publishing Company.

CONTENTS

WHAT ARE ROCKS AND MINERALS?

ROCKS MAKE up the hard, solid part of the earth's crust, or surface. In many places, the rocks are covered by soil, which contains tiny bits of rock. In other places, the rocks are covered by water.

There are many different kinds of rocks. All are made of solid chemical substances called minerals. The hardness, color, and weight of a rock depend on the minerals in it.

ROCK CYCLE

ROCKS change over time (below). Volcanoes thtow out molten rock, or magma. Magma becomes solid rock, which, over amny years, is eroded by the weather. Rivers carry the bits of rock to the ocean, where they settle on the ocean bed. There, the bits pile up and form new rocks. Heat inside the earth melts some rocks. Volcanoes throw them out as magma, restarting the never-ending rock cycle.

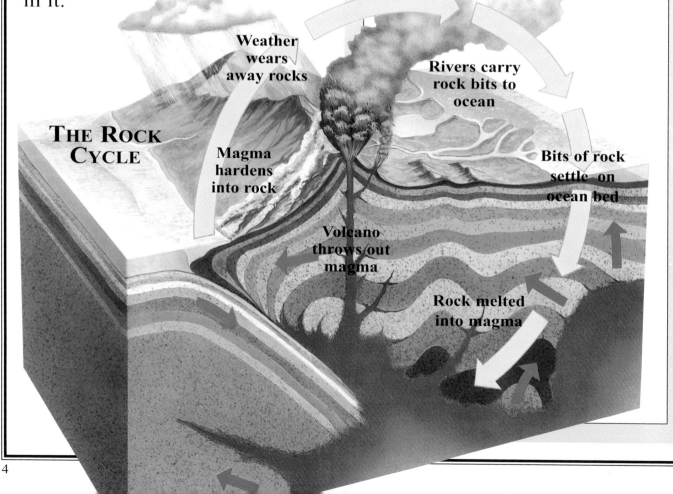

THE ROCK CYCLE

Weather wears away rocks

Rivers carry rock bits to ocean

Magma hardens into rock

Bits of rock settle on ocean bed

Volcano throws out magma

Rock melted into magma

ROCK STRATA

Rocks are formed in layers called strata. Huge forces inside the earth bend the layers. In coastal and mountain regions, the bent strata are sometimes exposed and show up as wavy lines.

GRANITE AND QUARTZ

THE close-up of granite rock above shows the different colors of its minerals. The light pink areas are minerals called feldspar. The darker, gray areas are quartz. The black spots are mica. The glassy, pink rock below is rose quartz. Quartz is one of the hardest and most common minerals.

IGNEOUS ROCKS

BENEATH THE earth's cool crust is a very hot layer, called the mantle, from which magma comes. When magma cools and hardens, it forms igneous rocks. Igneous means "fiery". Volcanoes spew some magma onto the earth's surface, where it cools. Other magma remains underground, where it cools very slowly to form rocks made up of large particles, or bits. Over millions of years, these underground rocks, called intrusive igneous rocks, may reach the surface as the rocks above them wear away.

WEARING AWAY

WIND and rain wore away the granite of Wave Rock (above), in Australia, to form a smooth, wave shape. Half Dome (left), in Yosemite National Park, USA, is a granite mountain 8,800 feet (2 700 meters) high. Its sheer slopes were carved by glaciers and rivers.

Granite

Pegmatite

Syenite

Gabbro

Peridotite

Diorite

INTRUSIVE IGNEOUS ROCKS

GRANITE is the most common kind of intrusive igneous rock found on the earth's surface. Each kind of intrusive igneous rock is made up of different types and amounts of minerals. Six kinds of intrusive igneous rocks are shown above.

BALANCING BOULDERS

Tors, such as the one in southwest England shown left, are towers of balancing boulders. The boulders were once surrounded by softer rocks. Over thousands of years, the softer rocks were gradually worn away by the weather.

VOLCANIC ROCKS

THE MAGMA that pours out of volcanoes onto the earth's surface is called lava. Hot lava cools and hardens to form a kind of rock called volcanic or extrusive igneous rock. Just like the intrusive kind, extrusive igneous rocks are made up of different minerals. These volcanic rocks are usually made up of smaller particles than rocks that form underground. Basalt is the most common kind of volcanic rock. Basalt forms from very runny lava, which usually flows a long way from a volcano.

LAVA ISLAND

ON the island of Iceland, water that has melted from glaciers plunges over tall formations of basalt rock (left). Iceland itself was formed over time by lava flowing from underwater cracks in the surface of the earth.

FIERY FOUNTAINS

Kilauea volcano (above), on the island of Hawaii, throws lava up into the air, making dramatic, fiery fountains. A river of lava flows from the volcano and later cools to form basalt. Kilauea is one of the most active volcanoes in the world.

Basalt

Andesite

Obsidian

Pumice

Tuff

EXTRUSIVE IGNEOUS ROCKS

FIVE kinds of volcanic rocks are shown above. The earth's surface is mostly basalt. Andesite is often found in the Andes Mountains. Obsidian looks dark and glassy. Pumice is full of air holes and very light. Tuff is made of volcanic ash.

DEVILS TOWER

Devils Tower (left) is a huge rock pillar in Wyoming, USA, made of magma forced close to the surface 50 million years ago. It was covered by layers of softer rock, but those outer rocks have since worn away.

SEDIMENTARY ROCKS

ROCKS THAT are exposed to the weather are slowly broken down into small particles. The particles are carried away by ice, water, or wind and settle on the bottoms of rivers, lakes, and oceans. Over thousands of years, layers of particles, called sediment, build up on top of one another. They are squeezed together and form new rocks. These rocks are called sedimentary rocks.

THE GREAT PYRAMID

WHEN it was built over 4,500 years ago, this Egyptian pyramid (right) was the world's tallest structure. It was made from more than two million blocks of hand-cut limestone.

LIMESTONE CAVES

MOST caves are found in areas of limestone, a soft sedimentary rock made of the skeletons and shells of sea animals. Over time, rainwater dissolves limestone to make caves. Water dripping through limestone creates the fantastic shapes of stalactites and stalagmites, shown left, in a cave in Tennessee, USA.

SANDSTONE ARCH

This arch (left) in Utah, USA, is made of a sedimentary rock called sandstone. Sandstone is made of grains of sand pressed together. It has taken millions of years for water and wind to create this arch.

Sandstone

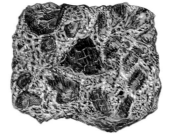

Limestone

Conglomerate

Breccia

Shale

KINDS OF SEDIMENTARY ROCK

Sandstone and limestone (above), are common kinds of sedimentary rocks. Conglomerates contain small pebbles, cemented together. Breccia is made up of large pieces of sediment. Shale is a hard rock made of mud or clay.

PAINTED HILLS

The Painted Hills (left), northwest of Mitchell in Oregon, USA, show layers of mudstone. This sedimentary rock forms from particles of clay. The Painted Hills are part of the John Day Fossil Beds National Monument.

CHANGED ROCKS

THE FORM of a rock can change if it is heated or squeezed enough when it is underground. Some rocks are baked by the hot magma below them. Others are squeezed by the weight of rocks above them or by the movement of the rocks around them. Rocks that change in form are called metamorphic. The particles in some metamorphic rocks are squeezed and become smaller. In others, the particles are stretched and become longer and thinner. Marble and slate are metamorphic rocks.

TAJ MAHAL

Over 350 years ago, about 20,000 workers built the beautiful Taj Mahal (above), in India. It is made of white marble and rests on a base of red sandstone. Marble is a changed form of limestone.

SPLITTING SLATE

SLATE is a changed form of shale. It is dug out of the ground, as in this mine (left), in England. Slate is made of fine grains of a mineral called mica. It can be split into thin sheets easily. The sheets, also known as slates, are used for roofing.

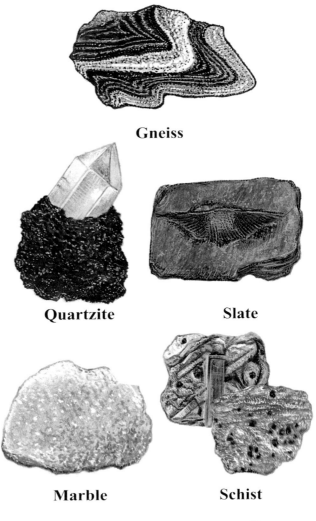

Gneiss

Quartzite

Slate

Marble

Schist

KINDS OF METAMORPHIC ROCK

GNEISS (above) forms from either igneous rocks, such as granite, or sedimentary rocks. Quartzite forms from sandstone. Slate forms if shale is under great pressure at low temperatures. At high temperatures, shale becomes schist.

MARBLE QUARRY

Marble is a metamorphic rock. The world's most famous marble quarry is at Carrara, in northern Italy (left). The great Italian artist Michelangelo (1475-1564) got white marble from this quarry for his beautiful sculptures.

GRAND CANYON

THE STEEP walls of the Grand Canyon, in Arizona, USA, give spectacular views of the earth's rock layers. The canyon was carved by the Colorado River, which, over thousands of years, eroded the land. In places the canyon, which is the deepest in the world, is 5,250 feet (1 600 meters) deep. The rock layers show some of the history of the earth's crust, because the rocks at the bottom of the canyon are 2,000 million years old – almost half the age of the earth.

ROCK LAYERS

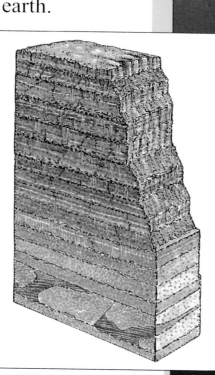

BILLIONS of years ago, the granite and schist rocks at the bottom of the Grand Canyon were an ocean floor. Over hundreds of millions of years, layers of sandstone, shale, and limestone built up on top of them.

Carving the Canyon

THE Colorado River flows through the Grand Canyon (above). Once there was no canyon. Then, about six million years ago, the river started to loosen the sandy gravel and carve out the canyon (see illustration below). Over millions of years, the river carved deeper and deeper into the rocks.

Millions of years ago

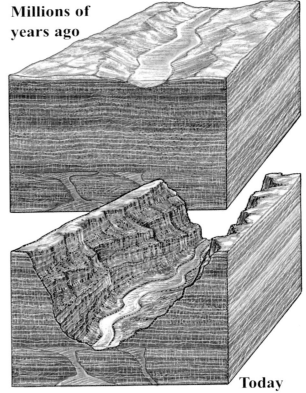

Today

AT THE SEASHORE

AS WAVES pound against the shore, they wear away rocks. Over many years, rocks from cliffs and other large coastal formations break off and fall down to the seashore. The waves then break the rocks down into smaller pieces. Water wears the pieces into round pebbles. Eventually, the pebbles are worn down into grains of sand, each less than $1/16$ inches (2 millimeters) across. There are even smaller grains, which we call silt and clay. These tiny particles are the raw materials from which future sedimentary rocks will form.

BOULDERS AND SAND
The sea is eroding the boulders on the beach of an island (above) in the South China Sea, near the coast of Malaysia. First the water will reduce them to small pebbles and then, eventually, to sand.

CHALK CLIFFS

THE sea wears away soft rocks, such as the chalk cliffs (left) in southern England, much more quickly than it erodes harder rocks such as granite. Chalk is a very white form of limestone and is made up of the remains of tiny sea animals and plants.

BLACK SAND

BLACK sandy beaches are made up of small grains of volcanic rock or ash. The two main volcanic rocks, basalt and andesite, are both very dark-colored. The beach above is on the Pacific coast of El Salvador. This Central American country has many active volcanoes.

THE TWELVE APOSTLES

The huge stacks of rock below, called the Twelve Apostles, stand just off the shore of southeast Australia. The pounding of the ocean waves created the stacks by wearing away the limestone cliffs. The Twelve Apostles stand where the earlier shoreline stood thousands of years ago. Today, seabirds nest among the rock stacks.

FOSSILS

FOSSILS ARE the remains of animals and plants that lived millions of years ago and have been preserved in rocks. Fossils teach us about the history of life on earth.

An animal fossil begins to form when the animal dies and is buried by sediment. Its body rots, leaving only its hard shell or bones. Over millions of years, the sediment becomes rock, and the shell or bones are replaced by minerals. The fossil is revealed if the rock wears away.

AMMONITE

Many fossils formed in sediment on the ocean floor. This means that fossils of shellfish and other ocean creatures are very common. The large fossil above is of a spiral shellfish, called an ammonite, that became extinct 65 million years ago.

COAL

PLANT fossils (left) are often found in coal. Coal is a sedimentary rock that began to form in prehistoric swamp forests (right), when dead trees and plants were buried in mud. Over millions of years, pressure turned the buried plants into peat and then coal, which we now mine for fuel.

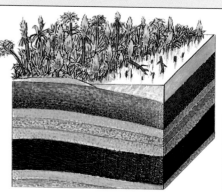

Swamp forest, about 300 million years ago

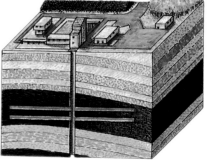

Coal mine, today

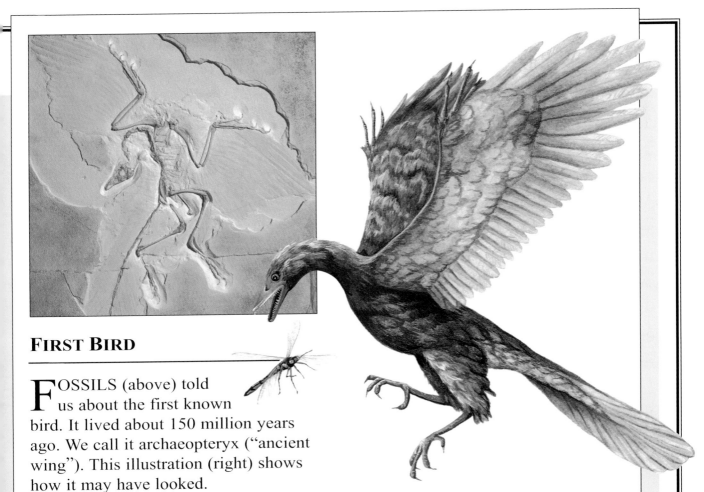

FIRST BIRD

FOSSILS (above) told us about the first known bird. It lived about 150 million years ago. We call it archaeopteryx ("ancient wing"). This illustration (right) shows how it may have looked.

DINOSAURS

THIS huge thigh bone (left) belonged to a camarasaurus. This plant-eating dinosaur was 59 feet (18 meters) long and lived about the same time as archaeopteryx. Fossil dinosaur eggs (below) have also been found.

MINERALS

ROCKS ARE made of minerals, and minerals are made of substances called elements. Most minerals consist of two or more elements. There are about 3,000 different minerals, but only about 100 of them are common. Minerals vary in their hardness, weight, color, and how they break. Some minerals form solid units called crystals, which have regular, geometrical shapes.

OPTICAL EFFECT

A mineral's color helps to identify it. Some minerals are transparent. Pure, clear, calcite (right) has a special property—it gives a double image of things seen through it. Most kinds of calcite, which is the main mineral in limestone, are white.

1. Talc   2. Gypsum   3. Calcite   4. Fluorite   5. Apatite

6. Feldspar   7. Quartz   8. Topaz   9. Corundum   10. Diamond

HARDNESS SCALE

ALMOST 200 years ago, the geologist Friedrich Mohs made up a scale to describe the hardness of minerals. He numbered ten minerals 1 to 10. Each can scratch a mark on minerals with lower numbers. Talc (1) is the softest mineral, and diamond (10) the hardest.

MINERALS IN CLOSE-UP

SCIENTISTS use special microscopes to study the make-up of rocks. This slice of basalt rock (right) shows several minerals— olivine (blue), pyroxene (yellow), and feldspar (gray).

HOT SPRINGS
At Mammoth Hot Springs, in Yellowstone Park, USA, there are amazing terraces of calcite mineral deposits. The spring water leaves calcite on the surface as it cools. The minerals build up over many years to form the terraces.

rogress through
onths and then,
n the ground in
rvested. Using a

to the st as
od grow, the
then so d by
, either two
one is r the
and h o dry
grey
red to be woven
several days t
product of thi

ORES

AN ORE is a rock or mineral that contains a useful metal. Ore deposits often occur in cracks, called veins, in rocks. Some metals, such as gold and silver, can be found pure in rocks. Most metals, however, such as aluminum and iron, are found mixed with other elements. Before they can be used, many metals must be extracted from the ore and refined by smelting, a process that heats and melts the ore.

ORE MINE, CHILE
After it is dug from the ground at this open-cast mine in the Andes (above), ore is crushed and smelted to extract copper.

MINING FOR GOLD

AT the mine above, in Brazil, workers mine gold by hand. They dig out rock, which they hope contains gold ore. Then they wash the rock in special containers. Any gold particles sink to the bottom of the containers.

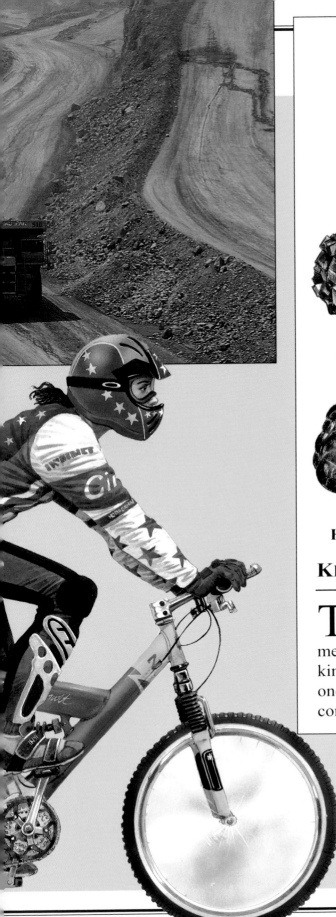

Chalcopyrite (copper)

Galena (lead)   **Bauxite (aluminum)**

 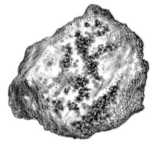

Hematite (iron)   **Cinnabar (mercury)**

KINDS OF ORES AND METALS

THE ores above produce the metals listed after them in brackets. Some metals, such as copper, are found in several kinds of ore. Some ores contain more than one metal. Galena, for example, often contains copper, gold, and silver.

LIGHT AND STRONG

Aluminum is a strong metal, especially when it is mixed with other metals. It is also one of the lightest metals and does not rust easily. These qualities make aluminum very good for bikes (left).

GEMSTONES

MINERALS THAT are especially beautiful and rare are called gemstones. Gemstones such as diamonds, rubies, sapphires, and emeralds are used in jewelry or as ornaments. They are rare because the conditions needed to form them—the right temperature and pressure, for example—are also rare. When they are mined, most gemstones have a rough texture and an irregular shape, giving little hint of their hidden beauty. To make them beautiful, they are cut and polished before being sold or made into jewelry.

OPAL MINE
The best opals come from Australia, and about half of these come from the mine at the town of Coober Pedy (above). Opals were first found there in 1911. Most

SPARKLERS

DIAMONDS (left) reflect light and break it up into many different colors. To give the greatest brilliance, diamonds are cut into stones with many facets, or sides. A "brilliant cut" diamond has 58 facets.

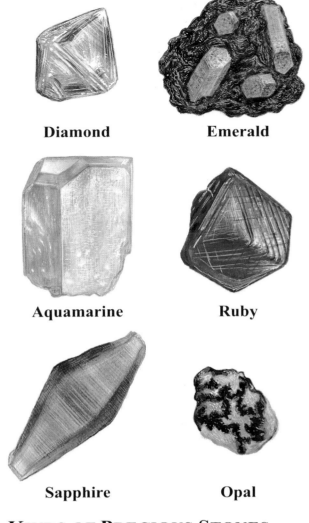

Diamond   Emerald

Aquamarine   Ruby

Sapphire   Opal

opals form in sedimentary rocks, but some form in holes in volcanic rocks. The gems can be many colors, and the most valued is black. Opal measures 6 on the Mohs scale.

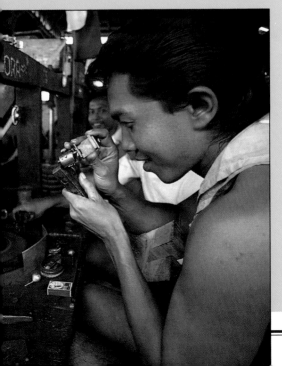

KINDS OF PRECIOUS STONES

EMERALD and aquamarine, shown above, are kinds of a mineral called beryl. They measure 7.5 to 8 on the hardness scale. Rubies and sapphires both are types of a mineral called corundum. They measure 9 on the hardness scale.

INDUSTRIAL USE

Diamonds make very useful cutting and grinding tools because they are the hardest naturally occurring substance. Usually it is only the imperfect, less valuable diamonds that are used in this way.

ROCKS FROM SPACE

THERE ARE billions of tiny rocks, called meteoroids, hurtling through our solar system. Millions of them enter the earth's atmosphere every day. We call them meteors or shooting stars. Most meteors burn up as they hit the atmosphere, but some reach the earth's surface. We call these rocks meteorites.

Every year, thousands of small meteorites arrive on earth, but most fall in the oceans or deserts. Scientists find only a few large rocks from space each year. There are three different kinds of meteorites—stony, iron, and stony-iron.

METEOR CRATER

Meteor Crater (below), in Arizona, USA, was made by a large iron meteorite about 50,000 years ago. The crater measures 4,180 feet (1 275 meters) wide and 570 feet (175 meters) deep.

METEORITE

THIS iron meteorite (left) is the largest ever found. Discovered in Namibia in 1910, it landed about 80,000 years ago. Huge meteorites such as this one often break into smaller pieces when they hit the ground.

ANTARCTICA

THOUSANDS of small meteorites have been found on the frozen continent of Antarctica (right). Scientists think some of them may have come from the Moon.

MARTIAN ROCK

THIS rock (right), found in Antarctica, is thought to have come from Mars. Some scientists believe it shows that life, in the form of bacteria, could once have existed on Mars.

USING ROCKS AND MINERALS

SCIENTISTS CALLED geologists study the structure of the earth and its rocks. They have learned much about our planet and its history.

Throughout history, people have used rocks and minerals in many different ways. At first they used rocks as tools, or crushed them to make colorful pigments. Since then, rocks have been used for building, ores have been mined, metals refined, and gemstones used for jewelry.

COLLECTING ROCKS

THESE scientists (left) are collecting rocks in Thailand. Scientists called mineralogists specialize in the study of minerals. Paleontologists study fossils found in rocks to learn about prehistoric plants and animals.

FLINT TOOLS

Thousands of years ago, humans made the first tools by striking lumps of flint to give them sharp edges. They saw that striking flint also produced sparks, and began using it to start fires.

DECORATION

THIS Guatemalan worker (above) is polishing jade. Two minerals, nephrite and jadeite, are called jade. Jade is translucent and mainly green. In Central America, jade was highly prized by the Maya people, who used it for beautiful jewelry.

CANADIAN NATIONAL TOWER

The CN Tower rises to 1,814 feet (553 meters) in the city of Toronto, Canada. Like many modern buildings, much of the tower is made of concrete. Concrete is a mixture of water with limestone, clay, sand, and gravel. Once it dries, concrete is very strong and durable.

GLOSSARY

Bacteria — Tiny one-celled organisms

Crust — The hard outer layer of the earth

Crystal — A solid form of mineral with a regular, geometrical shape

Element — A basic chemical substance

Extrusive — Describing igneous rocks that form on the earth's surface

Facet — One flat side of a cut gemstone such as a diamond

Fossil — The preserved remains of prehistoric animals and plants

Gemstone — A beautiful, rare mineral used in jewelry or as an ornament

Geologist — A scientist who studies the structure of the earth and its rocks

Glacier — A slowly moving mass of ice

Igneous — Describing rocks made from cooled magma beneath the earth's surface, or from solidified lava on the surface

Intrusive — Describing igneous rocks that form beneath the earth's surface

Lava — Magma that pours out of a volcano onto the earth's surface

Magma — Hot molten rock formed beneath the earth's surface

Mantle — The thick layer of hot rock beneath the earth's crust

Metamorphic — Describing rocks changed in form by great heat or pressure

Meteor — A meteoroid that enters the earth's atmosphere and makes the streaking light of a shooting star

Meteorite — A meteor that lands on the earth's surface

Meteoroid	A small rock moving through the solar system
Mineral	A solid chemical substance that occurs naturally in the earth
Mineralogist	A scientist who studies minerals
Ore	A rock or mineral containing a useful metal
Paleontologist	A scientist who studies fossils to learn about prehistoric animals and plants
Peat	The rotted vegetation of buried plants
Quarry	A place where rocks are dug out of the ground
Sediment	Rock particles and other matter that settle and build up in layers on land or the ocean floor
Sedimentary	Describing rocks formed from rock particles that have been deposited by ice, water, or wind
Smelting	A process of heating and melting ores to extract metal
Stalactite	A rock formation that hangs from the ceiling of a cave
Stalagmite	A rock formation that sticks up from the floor of a cave
Strata	Layers of rock
Translucent	Describing a substance that one can partly see through
Transparent	Describing a substance that one can see through
Volcanic rock	Igneous rock that forms on the earth's surface
Volcano	An opening through which molten rock comes from deep inside the earth

INDEX

12 13 14 15 16 17 18 19 20   Printed in the U.S.A 2 1 0 9 8 7 6 5